Contemplation Seeds from the Shariyat

ECKANKAR
Minneapolis
www.Eckankar.org

Contemplation Seeds from the Shariyat
Copyright © 2016 ECKANKAR

All rights reserved. No part of this book may be reproduced, stored in a retrieval system, or transmitted in any form by any means, whether electronic, mechanical, photocopying, recording, or otherwise, without prior written permission of Eckankar.

The terms ECKANKAR, ECK, EK, MAHANTA, SOUL TRAVEL, and VAIRAGI, among others, are trademarks of ECKANKAR, PO Box 2000, Chanhassen, MN 55317-2000 USA.

Printed in USA

Second printing—2016

Library of Congress Cataloging-in-Publication Data

Names: Klemp, Harold, selector of quotes.
Title: Contemplation seeds from the Shariyat.
Description: Minneapolis : ECKANKAR, 2016.
Identifiers: LCCN 2016006652 | ISBN 9781570434327 (pbk. : alk. paper)
Subjects: LCSH: Eckankar (Organization)--Doctrines.
Classification: LCC BP605.E3 S53 2016 | DDC 299/.93--dc23 LC record available at http://lccn.loc.gov/2016006652

♾ This paper meets the requirements of ANSI/NISO Z39.48-1992 (Permanence of Paper).

Introduction

The Shariyat-Ki-Sugmad, Eckankar's holy scripture, is a gift to the world. Each page of this powerful little book contains a specially selected quote from *The Shariyat*—a contemplation seed you can take into your spiritual exercises and nurture with loving attention. In doing so, you take another step in your journey home to the heart of God.

At the back of this book, you'll find a helpful guide to some of the spiritual terms that appear in these passages.

𝒯he scriptures of the Shariyat-Ki-Sugmad can be spoken and written on the lower planes. But in the higher worlds it is only the heavenly white music.

p. 2

*S*oul exists because God loves It.

p. 142

*S*oul is immortal, and Its future is the future of a thing whose growth and splendor has no limits.

p. 318

*T*he very heart of the doctrine of ECK is love. This love is that divine essence which unites all reality and brings together all Souls.

p. 126

*A*s threads in cloth are woven and interwoven, as the particles of water fabricate the sea, all things in the spiritual worlds and all things in the material worlds are woven and fashioned of the ECK.

p. 25

$\mathcal{T}$he Word, the Voice of the Sugmad, goes forth like a wave from the center of a pond and sings Its way through all the planes in many different songs and melodies.

p. 68

*L*ove comes to one in whom the Word has stirred. It is like the rushing of the mighty winds and the tongues of fire.

p. 9

𝒯he Living ECK Master always brings Light and Love into the world so that all men shall profit by them. Not just his own followers, but the world of itself.

p. 129

The words of the Mahanta alone can change the world, completely and irrevocably.

p. 186

𝒪nce Soul has made the slightest degree of contact with the Mahanta, there is never any parting between them. He becomes as close to his loved ones as their own heartbeat, as their own breathing.

p. 38

*T*he ECK chela is always cherished, beloved, and protected by the ECK Master in every act of the chela's life.

p. 211

*M*an does not have to become anything other than what he is in order to have divine guidance, divine protection, divine wisdom, and divine understanding through the Living ECK Master.

p. 155

Surrender to the Master, who is the instrument of the ECK, is the great pleasure of life.

p. 8

Heaven exists in all persons, and all persons have access to It.

p. 12

𝓘t is now, in the age of liberation from traditions and thought, that the ECK can become known to all persons.
p. 335

The ECK is rooted and grounded in all life—he, she, it, I, thee, and thou. It is here, there, and everywhere; permeating all directions, east, west, south, and north; above and below; everywhere, in all seasons.

p. 24

To the man who has touched the robe of God there is no distinction of race or belief, no consciousness of nationality, and no religious difference.

p. 32

*E*CK is the thread—so fine as to be invisible, yet so strong as to be unbreakable—which binds together all beings in all the worlds of God, in all universes, throughout all time, and beyond time into eternity.

p. 428

*W*hether they consciously realize it or not, all are actually the children of the ECK kingdom. In this way it makes no difference what religion or path Soul may adopt for Itself, It is a full citizen of the kingdom of ECK.

p. 190

The ECK is the Ocean of Love, a life-giving, creative sea, heard by the divine followers of the Sugmad.

p. 2

The sounds of the oceans, the whistling of the winds, the rustle of trees in the forests, the beating of drums, the noises of great cities, the cries of animals, and the words and emotional sounds of people are the natural elemental sounds of the ECK.

p. 225

𝒯he word is *HU*, the universal name of God, which is in the language of every living thing. It is everywhere, in everything.

p. 332

𝓘n this mantric sound all the positive and forward-pressing forces of the human, which are trying to blow up its limitations and burst the fetters of ignorance, are united and concentrated on the ECK, like an arrow point.

p. 333

$\mathcal{T}$he divine strain of God's music hums around man constantly, yet he is of such gross nature that he cannot hear It. Only by entering into the divine silence of the Spiritual Exercises of ECK, and closing his ears to the world of illusions, can he catch the celestial melody.

p. 386

𝒯ruth ... needs only an inward reverence and a willing ear to hear the divine music of God.

p. 386

$\mathscr{T}$he ECK is the root and background of all life, all religions and daily living. It is the principle by which all life, the entire universes of God go forward. It is truth, and it is beauty.

pp. 333–34

𝒯ruth, goodness, love, and beauty are commonly regarded as poetic ideas, but they are, in essence, spiritual facts.

p. 425

With the ECK comes the Sound of the flute of the Sugmad. This is what Soul is, and none can deprive Soul of It once It has been experienced.

p. 192

The ECKist knows the strange and beautiful ecstasy which comes of the union with the ECK.

p. 377

The ECK has existed throughout all eternity, yet from ancient times until now, from the beginning, the ECK has been presented under an endless number of names.... By what can you tell It? It is known only through your insights, your intuitions, your experiences with what is eternal, and what you know as truth.

p. 417

𝒯hose who follow the ECK take nothing for granted, for they must prove it for themselves.

p. 13

𝒯his time he recognizes the Mahanta as the one he has been searching for all these many lives. It comes upon him like a burst of the sun from behind a cloud following a storm.

p. 132

*A*ll life becomes a realization that the Mahanta is always present, and that the ECK makes life a joy to live. If the chela errs at any time there should be little need for discouragement, but one of joy, for he can now compare the errors with the joys of his life.

p. 252

𝒯here is never a time when the world is without a Mahanta, the Living ECK Master, for God manifests Itself again and again in the embodiment of the chosen one.

p. 112

*W*hat the Mahanta, the Living ECK Master teaches in words is only a fraction of what he teaches by his mere presence, his personality, and his living example.

p. 336

𝒯he one God, the Sugmad, exists only. All else is a part of Its beingness.

pp. 153–54

$\mathscr{E}$ach created form of life, by its own nature, longs for the perfection of the Sugmad.

p. 32

The Living ECK Master is . . . the divine man; a real son of God. Yet every man has in him the latent possibilities for the same expansion to mastership. He only requires the Living ECK Master to help develop it.

pp. 94–95

𝓗e accepts the aid and guidance of the Living ECK Master over a path which is unknown to himself.

p. 130

The kingdom of heaven is here with man constantly, in the very heart of those who realize God, and the whole purpose of life is to make God a reality.

p. 387

If you work, if you study, if you love, if you contemplate, and if you do any of these things for the love of truth or the love of the Sugmad, then, whether you know it or not, you are already practicing the works of ECK.

p. 405

𝒯o live in the world of humanity, as the chela must do until the end of his days in the physical embodiment, he must constantly dwell on the spiritual summits of God.

pp. 116–17

𝓘t is love and love only which will admit the seeker to all the heavenly worlds, for it is the golden coin which must be presented when entering the high regions of Spirit.

p. 312

The initiate has learned that by self-surrender he does not resist life, but goes along with it in an active manner. He is like the willow bough which is weighed down by the winter snow and does not resist but bends spontaneously under the weight so the snow falls off.
p. 472

The past is always put behind without regret, and the future, when plans have been made, left in God's hands.

p. 364

The chela must act as a channel for the ECK where it can best be done—at his job, in his home, and in his social environment. He is always working in silence, always open to let the ECK change all his life around him.

p. 179

What a man receives in contemplation, he must pour out in love.

p. 425

𝒯hose living in the state of selflessness will speak gently and carefully, selecting their words to give life to others.

p. 427

𝓘t is in the small events, such as goodness in the daily things of life, being kind to a child, speaking softly to those who can be hurt easily, noninjury to a fellow creature, and the giving of one's self to others who are without the essentials of life, that spiritual unfoldment can be found.

pp. 432–33

*E*very moment is known to be of infinite value, not because of what precedes or follows it, but because it is the moment of communication with God.

p. 363

𝓘f the karma of man has brought him nothing more than a capacity to love, then he has not lived in vain for a thousand past lives.

p. 313

$\mathcal{O}$nce you set your feet firmly on the path of ECK, you become the ideal and the standard by which all men are judged.

p. 417

$\mathcal{E}$ach initiate is a potential light of the world.

p. 479

Glossary of Spiritual Terms

chela A spiritual student, often a member of Eckankar.

ECK The Life Force, the Holy Spirit, the Sound Current which sustains all life.

HU (*HYOO*) The most ancient, secret name for God. It can be sung as a love song to God aloud or silently to oneself to align with God's love.

initiate A member of Eckankar who has received the linkup with the holy Sound Current.

Living ECK Master The spiritual leader of Eckankar. He leads Soul back to God. He teaches in the physical world as the Outer Master and in the spiritual worlds as the Inner Master.
Sri Harold Klemp became the Mahanta, the Living ECK Master in 1981.

Mahanta (*mah-HAHN-tah*) An expression of the ECK, the Spirit of God that is always with you. The highest state of consciousness known on earth, only embodied in the Living ECK Master.

Soul The True Self, an individual, eternal spark of God. The inner, most sacred part of each person. Soul is the creative center of Its own world.

Spiritual Exercises of ECK Daily practices for direct, personal experience with the Sound Current. Creative techniques using contemplation and the singing of sacred words to bring the higher awareness of Soul into daily life.

Sugmad (*SOOG-mahd*) A sacred name for God. It is the source of all life, neither male nor female, the Ocean of Love and Mercy.

For Further Reading and Study

The Shariyat-Ki-Sugmad
Book One

Through *The Shariyat-Ki-Sugmad* you will discover an answer to every human question ever yet, or to be, devised. Its pages tell what life really consists of and how to live it. Book One is the first section of these works, which was dictated by Fubbi Quantz, the great ECK Master.

The Shariyat-Ki-Sugmad
Book Two

Book Two is the second section of these sacred writings from the Temples of Golden Wisdom in the spiritual worlds. It was dictated by Yaubl Sacabi, the great ECK Master. The essence of God-knowledge is laid down here.

The Shariyat-Ki-Sugmad
Books One & Two

The special one-volume edition with a combined index is bound in soft, blue leather; the pages are gilt-edged and carefully stitched.

The Shariyat-Ki-Sugmad
Book One
Audiobook (CD)

The Shariyat-Ki-Sugmad, which means "Way of the Eternal," is the holy scripture of Eckankar. Enjoy listening to the ancient scriptures of God's love for you.

The Shariyat-Ki-Sugmad
Book Two
Audiobook (CD)

Deepen your understanding of Soul and Its service to God in this second book of Eckankar's holy scriptures.

Spiritual Exercises for the Shariyat, Book One
Harold Klemp

Spiritual gold awaits your discovery! Every exercise in this book is a portal to greater freedom, love, and self-mastery. Infinite opportunities for growth and wonder are at your fingertips.

Advanced Spiritual Living

Go higher, further, deeper with your spiritual exploration!

ECK membership brings many unique benefits and a focus on the ECK discourses. These are dynamic spiritual courses you study at home, one per month.

The first year of study brings *The Easy Way Discourses* by Harold Klemp, with uplifting spiritual exercises, CD excerpts from his seminar talks, and activities to personalize your spiritual journey. Classes are available in many areas.

Each year you choose to continue with ECK membership can bring new levels of divine freedom, inner strength to meet the challenges of life, and direct experience with the love and power of God.

Here's a sampling of titles from *The Easy Way Discourses*:

- In Soul You Are Free
- Reincarnation—Why You Came to Earth Again

- The Master Principle
- The God Worlds—Where No One Has Gone Before?

Find Out More

For free books and more information about Eckankar

- Visit www.Eckankar.org;
- Call 1-800-LOVE GOD (1-800-568-3463), ext. BK 128 (USA and Canada only); or
- Write to: ECKANKAR, Dept. BK 128, PO Box 2000, Chanhassen, MN 55317-2000 USA.

To order Eckankar books online, you can visit www.ECKBooks.org.

To receive your advanced spiritual-study discourses, along with other annual membership benefits, go to www.Eckankar.org (click on "Membership" then "Online Membership Application"). You can also call Eckankar at (952) 380-2222 to apply. Or write to the address above, Att: Membership.